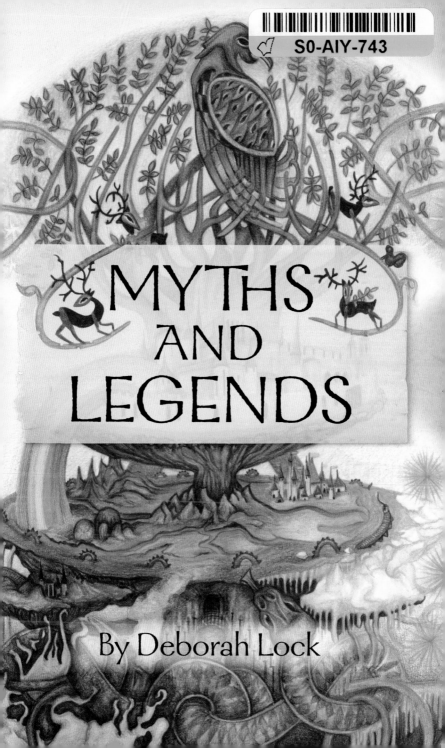

MYTHS
AND
LEGENDS

By Deborah Lock

Series Editor Deborah Lock
US Senior Editor Shannon Beatty
Editors Nishtha Kapil and Katy Lennon
Designer Emma Hobson
Illustrator Emma Hobson
Art Editor Yamini Panwar
Picture Researcher Sakshi Saluja
Producer, Pre-production Francesca Wardell
DTP Designers Syed Md. Farhan and Anita Yadav
Managing Editor Soma B. Chowdhury
Managing Art Editor Ahlawat Gunjan
Art Director Martin Wilson

Reading Consultant
Linda B. Gambrell, Ph.D.

First American Edition, 2015
Published in the United States by DK Publishing
345 Hudson Street, New York, New York 10014

15 16 17 18 19 10 9 8 7 6 5 4 3 2 1
001—271351—September/15

DK books are available at special discounts when purchased in bulk for sales promotions,
premiums, fund-raising, or educational use. For details, contact:
DK Publishing Special Markets,
345 Hudson Street, New York, New York 10014
SpecialSales@dk.com.

Printed and bound in China.

The publisher would like to thank the following for their kind permission to reproduce their photographs:
(Key: a-above; b-below/bottom; c-center; f-far; l-left; r-right; t-top)
4 Dreamstime.com: Jakub Krechowicz / Sqback (t). **5 Dreamstime.com:** Chromorange (t); Gino Santa Maria (c).
20 Dreamstime.com: Cowardlion (cr). **21 Getty Images:** The Washington Post (br). **34 Dreamstime.com:** Ensuper (b).
35 Dreamstime.com: Ensuper (t, b). **40 Dreamstime.com:** Kellydbrown (br); Martin Schlecht (cra); Renegate13 (bl).
41 Alamy Images: Prisma Archivo (t). **Dreamstime.com:** Dpikros (bl); Jcoll (clb); Gors4730 (cr). **64 Dreamstime.com:**
Kmiragaya (cla). **66 Dreamstime.com:** Ensuper (c, b). **67 Dreamstime.com:** Ensuper (t, c, b). **68 Alamy Images:** The Art
Archive (b). **69 Alamy Images:** The Art Archive (crb, cla). **78–79 iStockphoto.com:** duncan1890. **86 Dreamstime.com:**
Plengsak Chuensriwiroj (cr). **Getty Images:** Morten Falch Sortland (bl). **87 Dorling Kindersley:** Powell-Cotton Museum,
Kent (l). **90 Alamy Images:** Ivy Close Images (cl); Lebrecht Music and Arts Photo Library (br). **91 Alamy Images:**
Pictorial Press Ltd (tl). **Dreamstime.com:** Peeterson (br). **114 Dreamstime.com:** Du Zongjun (tr). **114–115 Dreamstime.
com:** Valentyna Chukhlyebova (c). **115 Dreamstime.com:** Jasmineforum (tr, cr). **117 Dreamstime.com:** Valentyna
Chukhlyebova (cr). **118 Dreamstime.com:** Jackq (b)
Jacket images: Front: Alamy Images: Life on white tr; Martin Siepmann / Westend61 GmbH cla;
Tosporn Preede b. iStockphoto.com: itsmejust ca.

All other images © Dorling Kindersley
For further information see: www.dkimages.com

A WORLD OF IDEAS:
SEE ALL THERE IS TO KNOW

www.dk.com

CONTENTS

All terms and names that have been included in the glossary and pronunciation guide are in bold text throughout the book.

WHAT IS A MYTH?

Myths are stories

Myths come from all over the world and are based on local traditions and legends. They often involve characters that have to overcome obstacles to complete exciting or dangerous journeys.

Myths are lessons

Myths help to explain how the world came into being. They give suggestions about how humans were created and how the natural world works, for example, why there is thunder, rain, night, and day. They also teach what behavior is right or wrong.

Myths are timeless

Myths were passed down from generation to generation through word of mouth. Myths are still being told today because of their meanings, lessons, and, in some cases, their religious message.

Myths are art

Characters from myths have been the subjects of many great works of art. From paintings and sculptures to theater and dance, these courageous, terrifying, or beautiful beings have influenced many different artistic pieces.

Myths are entertainment

Myths have been a popular form of entertainment for thousands of years and have influenced many of the stories that we read today. Myths have survived until now because they are exciting and grip the imagination of the reader.

Myths are not...

proven. No one knows where myths first came from. They have been passed through the centuries like a game of telephone. This means that small elements of the story will have changed with each telling.

CHAPTER 1

---✴---

Raven
(North American myths)

Imagine the world in darkness. A soft, cold darkness! Out of the darkness came a great snow-white bird. The bird was Raven. Raven flapped and flapped its white-feathered wings, pressing down the darkness. The compressed darkness formed solid earth. An icy black ocean surrounded the dark coastline.

People came to live along the coastline. They were pale and sickly. There was no warmth and nothing to eat. Raven flew over the land, seeding the land with its droppings.

Plants grew and the people chewed the nuts and leaves. Raven saw this wasn't providing enough food for them to survive.

Raven broke off a branch from an alder tree and shook it over the ocean. The leaves drifted down to the still water, and were sucked under the surface. The water began to bubble and bubble. The surface boiled vigorously and then stopped. As the water settled, fish began to jump and swim around. Raven had given the people fish to eat.

"Here comes the Raven who sets things right," they cried.

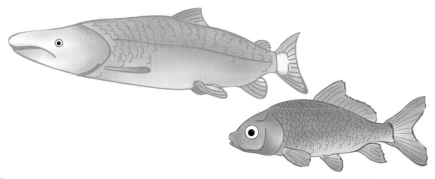

Raven saw that the people were thirsty. They longed for fresh water. They could not drink the water from the ocean because it was too salty. Raven knew there was one clear, fresh spring, but a greedy man named Ganook had built his house around it. Raven went to visit Ganook. Ganook was pleased to see Raven since he didn't get many visitors.

As they sat by the fire talking, Raven asked for a drink. Ganook showed Raven the shimmering crystal water flowing out from the rock.

"Don't drink it all," Ganook warned.

"It's the only fresh water in the entire world."

Raven drank and drank until bursting.

"Hold on!" cried Ganook.

"I just took a sip," Raven replied, staggering.

Back around the fire, Raven told Ganook a story. A long, dull story! Ganook's eyes began to close as Raven droned on. Raven darted to the spring to drink some more, but Ganook awoke.

"Where are you Raven?" he asked.

"I just took a stroll," Raven replied, returning to the fire to continue its story.

Raven spoke softly. Ganook fell asleep and snored. Quietly, Raven went to the spring and drank and drank until the spring was dry.

? QUESTION
Why did Raven tell
a long, dull story? ?

As Raven took the last drop, Ganook opened his eyes. He sprang to his feet and picked up his heavy wooden club to stop Raven. Raven tried to take off, but couldn't due to the weight of all the water. Raven ran clumsily around the room, chased by Ganook. With one desperate flap, Raven just managed to lift off, but the only way out was through the hole for the fire's smoke.

Flames scorched the white feathers, as Raven struggled to fly up the smoke hole. Raven's feathers turned black. At the top, Raven became stuck, too full of water to move. Ganook threw more logs on the fire. The thick smoke rose almost choking Raven to death.

With a mighty heave, Raven emerged
into the dark night, with feathers as black as
the sky. Too full of water to fly straight, Raven
wobbled and twisted, spurting water from its
beak here and there.

From the drops, trickling streams, salmon
pools, narrow creeks, and winding rivers
were formed.

The people drank, bathed, and splashed in
the cool, fresh water.

"Here comes the Raven who sets things
right," they cried.

The world was still cold and dark. Raven saw that the people couldn't see where they were going or what they were doing. To hunt and fish and even find berries, people had to reach out and feel for familiar trees, rocks, pools, and bumps in the ground.

There was no light because the Sky Chief kept it hidden away in a box. This box he kept close to him in his big house. Raven knew the people needed that light.

Raven turned into a tiny pine needle. When the chief's beautiful daughter went to a nearby stream to collect water, Raven drifted on the breeze and dropped into her jug. When she drank the water, the pine needle slipped smoothly down her throat.

Once inside her, Raven changed into a human baby and waited to be born. A while later, the chief's daughter gave birth to a boy with raven-black hair. The boy had shiny black eyes, a beaky nose, and a harsh, crowlike cry. The Sky Chief was delighted with the child and did everything he could to make him happy.

For many weeks, Raven lived as a gurgling baby, playing with his mother and his grandfather in their house. One day, Raven-boy caught sight of the hidden box and reached out to grab it. The Sky Chief snatched it away quickly, but the baby cried and cried and cried. His adoring grandfather gave in and handed over the box.

Immediately, Raven opened the box and let out the magic ball of light. Instantly, Raven turned back into a bird, picked up the ball in its beak, and flew out through the house's smoke hole. Raven flew high, passing over many mountains, rivers, and oceans. As Raven grew weary, half the light dropped and shattered into a thousand pieces. These became the stars and the Moon. The people could now see in the dark.

Eventually, completely exhausted, Raven let go of all the remaining light and it filled the sky. The precious light had turned into the Sun. The people rejoiced and danced in the Sun's warm rays. After this day, the Raven was forever known as the one who sets things right.

RAVEN'S REST BIRD SANCTUARY

Here at Raven's Rest we do our best to provide a loving home for all the weary ravens that were once the stars of myths and legends. Please feel free to look around and read about the ravens. Each has its own story to tell. However, be careful, some of them can give you a nasty peck!

APOLLO'S RAVEN

Once upon a time, this raven belonged to Apollo. It had white feathers until Apollo cursed it as punishment for bringing him bad news. This curse turned its feathers black.

KUTKH, RUSSIAN RAVEN SPIRIT

This raven is a cunning trickster and has flown in and out of many Russian legends. It helped with the creation of the world and also learned how to be a powerful shaman (witch doctor).

RAVEN FROM THE TOWER OF LONDON

This raven was one of the six guardian ravens of the Tower of London. Their job is to live in and protect the Tower. Legend says that if the ravens fly away, the Tower will crumble and a great disaster will fall upon England.

HUGINN AND MUNINN, ODIN'S RAVENS

The raven on the left-hand side below is named Huginn, which means "thought." On the right is Muninn, which means "memory." These two were once the faithful companions of the great Norse god **Odin**, the god of war. They served as his eyes and ears and spent their time perching on his shoulders.

PATHFINDER

Welcome to Pathfinder Pets. We specialize in matching our customers with the perfect spirit guide to help and advise them on their journey through life. We believe that all animals have spirits with special qualities. When a person feels a special connection with an animal it becomes their spirit guide or **totem**, which will protect and teach them valuable lessons.

TURTLE

Proving that slow and steady can win the race, this hard-shelled spirit sidekick symbolizes independence, protection, and security.

WOLF

This canine has lots of character and is always the leader of the pack. This furry spirit symbolizes intelligence and family values.

RAVEN

If a high-flying friend is what you require, take to the skies with this feathered companion. Symbolizing secrecy and courage this spirit animal will always be around to listen to you and guard your deepest secrets.

DEER

This graceful spirit is a calm comrade who will often give its owner an affectionate nuzzle. It is a kind and gentle guide who is always happy to lend a helping hoof.

SHAPESHIFTERS

THE TOKYO TRIBUNAL

NINE-TAILED FOX SEEN IN TOKYO

Tokyo residents have reported seeing a nine-tailed fox skulking around central Tokyo.

Local grocers have spied the animal making off with fruit from their stalls and rifling through garbage cans in the dead of night.

The nine-tailed fox has been present in Japanese legends for many years. The creature is named Kitsune and is said to be a shapeshifter, able to morph from a fox into a human. The question remains whether the myth is true and this really is the fabled Kitsune or if this is just a normal fox looking for food on the streets of Tokyo. Residents are warned to be cautious and not to approach the animal if they encounter it.

THE ORKNEY ORACLE

STRANGE CREATURE SPOTTED OFF THE COAST OF SCOTLAND

Local fishermen have reportedly sighted a strange seallike animal off the coast of the Orkney islands.

This elusive sea creature has been the topic of many Scottish legends. Folklore states that selkies look like seals when they are in water but can shed their skin and turn into humans. If their skin is found they will transform back into a seal and swim away.

Without photographic evidence it is difficult to say whether these sightings are indeed of the slippery selkie. Marine biologists are currently keeping watch over the waters in an attempt to track the animal.

Residents of the islands have been told to keep their eyes peeled in case a secretive selkie does sneak up on them.

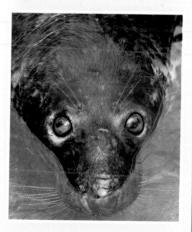

CHAPTER 2

Anansi
(West African myths)

Have you ever played a trick on someone? Sometimes it goes well, but at other times you get caught. There was once a wealthy young man named Anansi. He was crafty. He was greedy. He played tricks.

One day, he went to his father, the creator god, **Nyame**, and asked for an ear of corn.

"I'll repay you with one hundred servants," promised Anansi. Amused to know how Anansi would be able to do that, Nyame gave him the ear of corn.

Anansi went to the chief of an African village. "I need a safe place to keep my sacred ear of corn, given to me by Nyame, and to rest for the night," he requested. Anansi was treated very well and he was shown a hiding place for the corn. But that night, Anansi fed the corn to the chickens.

In the morning, Anansi cried, "Who stole the sacred corn? Nyame will punish you all." In fear, the villagers gave him a bushel of corn.

On the road, Anansi met a man with a chicken and exchanged the bushel for it. He went on to the next village.

"I need a safe place to keep my sacred chicken given to me by Nyame and rest for the night," he demanded. Again, Anansi was treated very well and he was shown a safe place for his chicken. But that night, Anansi killed the chicken and smeared the blood and feathers on the chief's door.

In the morning, Anansi cried, "Who killed the sacred chicken? Nyame will punish you all." The frightened villagers gave him ten of their best sheep.

On the road, Anansi met a man carrying
a dead body and swapped the sheep for it.
He went on to the next village.

"We need a place to rest. This is the son of
Nyame, who is already asleep," said Anansi,
pointing to the body. Anansi was treated like
royalty with a great feast.

In the morning, Anansi cried, "I cannot
wake the son of Nyame. You have killed him!
Nyame will destroy you all." The terrified
villagers told Anansi to pick one hundred of
their best men, take them to Nyame, and appeal
to save them.

So Anansi returned to Nyame, having turned
one ear of corn into one hundred servants.

One day, Anansi was tending his large field of crops when a ram came to graze. Anansi threw a rock, hitting it between the eyes and killing it instantly. As he gazed at the dead ram, Anansi recognized it as the finest in the world. It was the prized possession of an African king. Anansi knew that the king would be furious, so he would need a cunning plan.

He hung the dead ram on a nut tree and then told a spider about the tree with the most wonderful tasty nuts. The spider began spinning webs all around the ram. Anansi went to the king and told him that a spider must have killed his ram. The king thanked Anansi and offered him a great reward.

Over lunch, the king told his wife.

She laughed and said, "A spider's thread is not strong enough to kill a ram. It couldn't even lift the ram up! Anansi killed your ram."

Immediately, the angry king sent his soldiers to fetch Anansi. Anansi, thinking he was going to collect his reward, willingly went to the palace. In a rage, the king attacked Anansi, shattering him into pieces. Anansi was no longer a man but a spider with two body parts and eight long legs.

Anansi discovered that he could be even more cunning as a spider. He spun a web ladder up into the sky to spy on Nyame. There he spotted a wooden box.

"What's in the box?" Anansi asked.

"All the stories of the world," replied Nyame.

"I would like them," Anansi requested.

"If you can capture Hornet, whose sting is red hot, Python, who can swallow a goat whole, Leopard, who has teeth as sharp as spears, and Fairy, who has a terrible temper, and bring them to me," challenged Nyame, "then you can have all the stories as a reward."

Anansi worked out his plan and then set out to find Hornet. Anansi took with him a gourd filled with water. He threw the water over Hornet's nest. A black cloud of hornets swarmed out of the nest.

"Quick!" called Anansi. "It's raining! Come inside my nice, dry gourd to shelter."

Once all the hornets had flown inside,
Anansi wove a thick web across the opening.
Hornet was trapped.

Anansi went to look for Python, taking with
him a long branch. Anansi knew that Python
was proud. As he approached Python's tree,
Anansi began muttering loudly, as if to himself.

"What are you mumbling about?" asked
Python, overhearing.

QUESTION
Why did Anansi throw
water over Hornet's nest?

"Well, my wife thinks you are shorter than this branch, but I think you are longer," said Anansi. "I don't know how to convince her."

"Well there's a simple solution to that matter," said Python, unraveling himself. "I'll lie along the branch and prove that I am longer."

Python stretched himself out along the branch. Anansi quickly bound the snake with his silken thread so Python could not move.

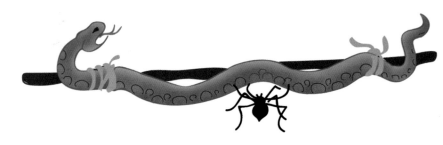

Anansi went on to find Leopard. He knew that Leopard walked down a certain path every night. So Anansi dug a deep hole across the path and then carefully covered it with branches and leaves. Anansi was exhausted and returned home to rest.

The next day, Anansi returned to the pit. As he drew close, he could hear scrabbling. Leopard had fallen in.

"Help! Someone help me!" Leopard cried.

"If I help you, will you promise not to eat me?" said Anansi. Leopard agreed.

Anansi tied one end of his thread to the top of a nearby tree, bending it down over the pit, and spun another thread from the tree down into the pit.

"Tie the end to your tail," instructed Anansi. Once fastened, Anansi released the treetop, and as the tree sprung back, Leopard whooshed into the air. As Leopard dangled against the tree, Anansi wrapped the beast up in thread, tightly.

Finally, Anansi set off to catch Fairy. Anansi carved a wooden doll, covered it in sticky gum and left it by a tree. He placed some yam on a plate beside the doll, and then spun a thread to the top of the doll's head and went to hide nearby. Fairy came along and seeing the doll and the yam asked, "Hello, little gum baby. May I have some yam?"

Anansi pulled the thread and the doll nodded. Fairy ate the yam and then said, "Thank you."

The doll stayed still. Angrily, the Fairy repeated, "I said THANK YOU. Answer me or I will make you cry."

Receiving no response, Fairy reached out to pick up the doll. As soon as Fairy touched it, she stuck fast. Anansi swiftly bound her in his sticky thread, too.

Nyame was delighted when he saw Anansi's success. He handed over the box with all the stories and Anansi brought them down into the world. He shared them with everyone, so that people would always have stories to tell.

TRICKSTERS

Watch out! There are tricksters on the loose! These mischievous characters have no sense of right or wrong, and will use cunning and deceit to get their own way. They will sometimes do things for the good of humans but often they just want to have fun.

WARNING!

— COYOTE —

American trickster, Coyote, is on the prowl. Do not approach this masterful mammal—he is cunning and dangerous.

There are many stories about Coyote's high jinks, for example, when he allowed the stars to escape, creating the Milky Way.

BEWARE!

— LOKI —

This shape-shifting god is a deceitful character who has many disguises. Just remember that you can't always trust what you see!

Brother to Odin, the Norse god of war, Loki is a fierce god with a large appetite; he once killed a dwarf to steal his food.

ATTENTION!

—TENGU—

Approach this Japanese spirit with extreme caution. A child of the god of storms, Tengu is part bird, part man.

Trained in martial arts, this spirit is a force to be reckoned with. Tengu plays tricks on Buddhist monks and robs the temples of those who disrespect him.

ANANSI WHO?

Anansi has spun his web far and wide and his stories have traveled all over the globe. He is known by many different names including Hanansi, Bre-Nancy, Kweku Anansi, and Baba Nancy. However, he is almost always represented as a spiderlike creature that enjoys getting into mischief and his tales are still told to this day.

NORTH AMERICA
In America, Anansi was called "Aunt Nancy." In these stories, he became female and was half spider, half woman. Several Native American tribes associate spiders with the important art of weaving and many believe it is bad luck to kill them.

CARIBBEAN
In the 16th century, people were taken from Africa to the Caribbean to work on the sugar **plantations**. The stories of Anansi went with them across the seas and the word of Anansi began to spread. The stories gave hope to those who had been enslaved. The African slaves told tales of rebellion and how wit and cunning could defeat power.

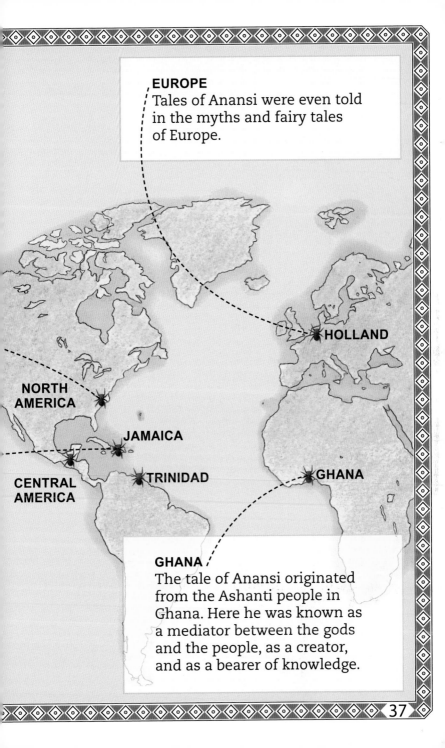

EUROPE
Tales of Anansi were even told in the myths and fairy tales of Europe.

HOLLAND

NORTH AMERICA

JAMAICA

CENTRAL AMERICA

TRINIDAD

GHANA

GHANA
The tale of Anansi originated from the Ashanti people in Ghana. Here he was known as a mediator between the gods and the people, as a creator, and as a bearer of knowledge.

CHAPTER 3

The Voyage of Odysseus

(Ancient Greek myths)

This next tale is about an epic sea voyage—a voyage that lasted more than a couple of weeks, and even more than a couple of months. It took ten long years. Our travelers are King **Odysseus** and his fleet of 12 ships with crew. They are returning victorious to their island home of Ithaca, after the ten-year Battle of Troy. The voyage shouldn't have taken them that long, but this tale is a warning never to offend the ancient Greek gods.

Spirits were high as the Ithacans set sail for

home. Troy had finally been defeated due to the cunning idea of their leader, Odysseus. It was his idea to build and leave the Trojan horse packed with Greek soldiers outside the city gates as a token of surrender. The Trojans fell for the trick and took the horse inside their city. While they celebrated, the Greek army returned and were let into the city by the soldiers.

Odysseus looked forward to seeing his wife Penelope and his son Telemachus once again. But trouble was ahead. On the request of the warrior goddess Athena, the sea god **Poseidon** summoned a storm to destroy most of the returning Greek's fleet. This was in revenge for the destruction of Troy, however Odysseus and his ships were spared because Athena favored him.

GREEK GODS FAMILY TREE

Ancient Greeks believed that there was a family of powerful giants who lived in the Heavens. These **immortal** gods were called Titans and had incredible strength and power. They took an interest in human life and often influenced events on Earth for their own enjoyment and gain. Here are some of them.

URANUS
Father Sky
His children included the 12 Titans, Cyclopes, and Giants.

APHRODITE
Goddess of love and beauty

HADES
God of the underworld

HESTIA
Goddess of the home

POSEIDON
God of the seas

DEMETER
Goddess of agriculture

GAIA
Mother Earth
Born out of the chaos at the beginning of creation, she married her first son, Uranus.

TITANS
Uranus and Gaia had 12 children known as the Titans, their names were: Oceanus, Tethys, Hyperion, Theia, Coeus, Phoebe, Cronus, Rhea, Mnemosyne, Themis, Crius, and Lapetus.

ZEUS
God of Heaven and Earth

HERA
Goddess of marriage

ATHENA
Goddess of wisdom and war

APOLLO
God of light, music, and healing

HERMES
God of trade and protector of travelers

After battling against the strong winds,
Odysseus and his crew stopped to raid the
city of Ismarus. Still victorious and jubilant,
Odysseus's crew plundered the city. They
were ruthless and greedy! Odysseus ordered
his men back to the ships with the loot, but
they refused. They wanted
to stay longer, drinking and
feasting. The angry people
in the neighboring towns
raised an army and drove
the Ithacans out.

Six men from
each ship
were killed.
As the fleet rounded
the tip of Greece, the
king of the gods, Zeus,
sent a nine-day stormy
wind that drove the ships
off course. Exhausted,
the fleet harbored when

they saw land. Unknown to them, this was the land of the Lotus-eaters. Anyone who ate from the lotus plant forgot everything. Unaware, Odysseus sent a small group of men to investigate. The local people offered them the intoxicating, delicious lotus fruit. As soon as they ate, they lost all thoughts about returning home.

"More fruit, more!" they cried.

Odysseus was horrified when he discovered the group. "Drag them back to the ships and lock them in the hold," he ordered the rest of his crew. It was a struggle pulling, lifting, and holding down the drugged men but finally they were on board. They set sail once again into the murky night.

"We're hungry!" groaned the crew. Food supplies were running low. Odysseus knew he needed to land again soon before his crew became restless.

As daylight dawned, a land with goats roaming wild came into view. Once anchored, they went ashore to catch a few for a meal. After eating, Odysseus and his men set out to find further supplies for the voyage. They hadn't gone far when they spotted a cave full of sheep and crates of milk and cheese. A vast boulder was rolled aside next to the large opening. The crew knew that only the strongest of all mythical creatures could move a boulder like that—a giant!

"Let's grab some food and hurry back," the crew urged Odysseus.

But their leader had other thoughts. "If we met the owner, I'm sure I could exchange some food for some of our wine." They all waited nervously for the cave dweller to return. The ground shook as he approached.

A mean-looking one-eyed Cyclops stood at the entrance. It was **Polyphemus**, the son of Poseidon. His one eye peered down at the cowering sailors.

Annoyed, Polyphemus devoured two men, and rolled back the boulder, trapping Odysseus and his crew inside. They needed an escape plan.

"We'll wait until morning," Odysseus said cunningly. "While Polyphemus herds his sheep, we will sharpen the long wooden log we've found. Then I'll get him drunk on his return and we'll blind him with it."

All went according to plan. That evening, Polyphemus drank and drank until he was drunk.

"What's your name?" he asked Odysseus.

"Outis," (which means "nobody" in Greek) he replied to protect his identity and his crew.

Once the Cyclops was asleep, Odysseus and his men plunged the stake into his single eye. Polyphemus cried out and the other Cyclopes came running. "Nobody is killing me," he told them. They went away thinking he was crazy.

In the morning, the blinded Polyphemus had to let his sheep out to graze. The crew strapped themselves to their bellies and escaped. Safe on board the ship with Polyphemus's flock, Odysseus proudly shouted back his real name.

Polyphemus, unable to reach them, cried out to his father Poseidon to avenge this trickery. Odysseus and his men were cursed.

Their next stop was the island of **Aeolia**. They were welcomed by the Keeper of the Winds, Aeolus, and stayed a few days as guests.

As they left, Aeolus gave Odysseus a leather bag. This contained all the strong winds that would prevent them from reaching home.

"Do not open the bag," Aeolus warned. He ordered a fair west wind and for nine days, the ships sailed straight. As Ithaca came into sight, Odysseus finally rested. However, his greedy men thought that the bag contained gold and precious valuables. Wanting a peek, they opened the bag, causing all the strong winds to escape.

Once again blown a long way off course, they arrived at the city of **Telepylus** at dawn. Odysseus sent all but his own ship into the harbor and a small group of men into the city to find out if the people were friendly. The group went to the palace where they were attacked and eaten by giants. Two escaped to warn the ships, but

the whole city of giants was now awake.
The giants threw large rocks at the fleet in
the harbor, destroying them all and killing
and feasting on the crew.

Helpless, Odysseus ordered his own ship
to sail away.

Disheartened and tired, the remaining survivors looked for a place to rest. They arrived at the island of Aeaea. This was the home of the immortal and powerful **sorceress** Circe.

Odysseus sent 12 men ashore. They wandered through the thick woods to the palace. Tame wolves, bears, and lions met them, wagging their tails in welcome. They led the men to Circe.

"Greetings," said Circe smiling. "Please join me for a feast."

The men ate hungrily but the food was drugged with poison that changed them into pigs.

Realizing that his men had vanished, Odysseus went to find them. On the way, the messenger god Hermes met him. Hermes gave him a plant that would stop Circe's spells from working and also some useful advice that would charm her.

As Odysseus greeted Circe, she tried to cast a spell on him but it failed. He drew his sword and threatened to kill her. From a prophecy, Circe knew that she would be charmed by the one who was immune to her magic. Circe relented and changed Odysseus's crew back to men. They stayed on the island, living in luxury.

As the year passed, Odysseus's crew became more and more eager to get on their way home again. Eventually they managed to persuade Odysseus to leave. But which way was home?

Odysseus asked Circe for directions.

"You must sail to Hades, the land of the dead, and speak to the spirit of the prophet **Tiresias**," she advised. "Sail to the shores of the River of Ocean, sacrifice a black sheep to lure the spirit, and then give the spirit a drink from the blood so that he may talk."

Odysseus followed these instructions and the ghostly spirit of Tiresias appeared and began to speak.

"Odysseus, king of Ithaca, you are cursed! Poseidon is punishing you for blinding his son Polyphemus. Once you return home, you must take a new journey to make peace with him. If you and your men wish to reach home, do not eat the cattle belonging to the sun god Helios on the island of Thrinacia. If you follow these warnings, you will die an old man."

As Tiresias's spirit faded, other spirits of his dead family and friends appeared to speak to Odysseus. But soon, he found himself surrounded by ghosts. In fear, Odysseus fled to his ship and sailed back to Circe's island.

DIALOGUE WITH THE DEAD

When Odysseus made his trip to Hades, he didn't realize just how many old friends he was going to encounter. Odysseus spoke with many ghosts and among these were: Elpenor, one of his crew members whom he didn't know was dead; **Agamemnon**, commander of the Greek Army in the Trojan War; and **Achilles**, a great warrior.

AGAMEMNON

Odysseus: "Agamemnon, my dear friend, what an honor it is to see you again. In life you were a king among men. What stroke of fate brought you to this realm of the dead?"

Agamemnon: "The treacherous **Aegisthus** stole my wife when I was fighting in Troy. Upon my return, he invited me to a grand banquet where I was to discover their betrayal. Aegisthus and my wife murdered me that day."

ACHILLES

Odysseus: "Achilles, one of the greatest warriors to walk the Earth. No man has been more blessed than you. Tell me, do you now rule among the un-living?"

Achilles: "Odysseus, this land of shadows is a punishment for me. I would rather be a lowly peasant on Earth where I might feel the sun on my face, instead of being shut away down here as lord of the lifeless dead."

ELPENOR

Odysseus: "Elpenor, I am shocked to see you! You have always been an important member of my crew. Why do you occupy a space in this gloomy land?"

Elpenor: "I was lost on Circe's island. Drunk from the wine and food, I fell from the roof and did not survive. My ghost then descended to the House of Hades."

After talking to Tiresias, Odysseus was eager to continue his voyage. Before he set sail, Circe warned him of other dangers ahead.

"Beware of the sirens," she told him urgently. "They are sea **nymphs** who lure sailors to their deaths with their sweet singing. Also sail swiftly past the monster, Scylla, to avoid the whirlpool of the monster **Charybdis**."

Odysseus ordered his men to plug their ears with beeswax. However, he wished to hear the sirens' song for himself.

"Tie me to the ship's mast," he instructed his men, "and don't untie me, no matter how earnestly I beg."

The sailors did as they were commanded before sailing away from Circe's island.

The sea was sparkling and calm and there was a light wind, which rippled the sail. As the sailors rowed, the sound of the sirens' song soon reached Odysseus's ears.

It was so temptingly beautiful. He couldn't resist their call and shouted out to the sailors to change direction toward the rocks from which the sound came. He struggled to free himself from his ropes. He cried out to be untied, but his sailors only tightened the bonds even more and rowed on past the island.

Next, the ship came to a narrow channel with tall cliffs on each side. Scylla, the fearsome six-headed sea creature, lived on one side and the great whirlpool of the monster Charybdis churned on the other side. Both couldn't be avoided.

Remembering Circe's words, Odysseus guided his ship against the cliffs where Scylla lived in her lair. The whole ship would be destroyed if it were sucked into the whirlpool.

"Row fast!" he shouted as the six heads of Scylla swooped down over the ship. Six sailors cried out as they were snatched and swallowed up. With hearts pounding, the sailors rowed on before Scylla came back for another mouthful.

Eventually, they saw Thrinacia, the island of the sun god. Odysseus did not want to stop but his crew was tired and demanded a rest. He warned them not to kill the oxen and they promised to obey. Once landed, a storm prevented them from leaving. At first, the crew happily ate the food supplies on the ship but then these began to dwindle. As Odysseus slept, the crew killed some oxen. The sun god was furious and asked Zeus to punish them.

As Odysseus's ship set sail from Thrinacia, Zeus created another storm with his thunderbolt. Lightning flashed, and the huge crashing waves destroyed the ship. All the crew except Odysseus were swept away and drowned.

Clinging onto a broken beam of his ship, Odysseus floated and drifted, eventually reaching the island of **Ogygia**. Here the beautiful goddess Calypso lived. With no ship, Odysseus settled down to live. Often he would look out to sea, wondering if he would ever reach home. For eight years, he waited.

On Mount Olympus, the goddess Athena summoned the gods together when Poseidon was away. "Zeus, Hera, brothers, and sisters, surely Odysseus has suffered enough. He should be allowed to return home. His wife is in trouble and his son has gone in search of him." They agreed.

Calypso helped Odysseus make a ship and he set sail once again. Poseidon saw this and caused a mighty storm. The ship was destroyed but Odysseus swam for two days protected by a sea goddess. He was washed ashore on the island of the Phaeacians. He told them his story and they rowed him home to Ithaca.

Odysseus's sea adventure was over but further trials lay ahead before he finally reclaimed his throne and was once again reunited with his wife and son.

ODYSSEUS'S JOURNEY

Here is a map showing possible locations of the places that Odysseus and his crew visited on their journey home.

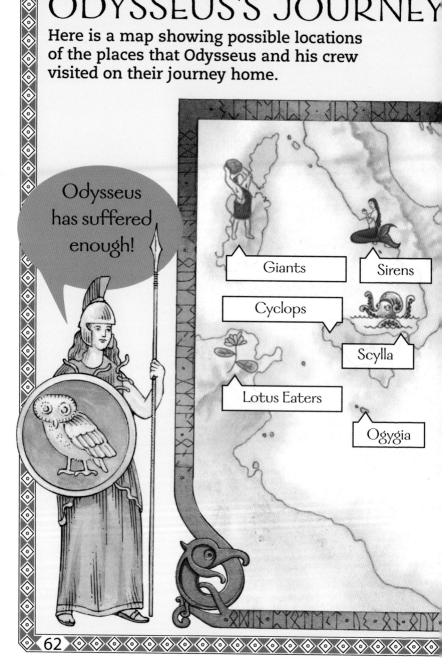

Odysseus has suffered enough!

Giants

Sirens

Cyclops

Scylla

Lotus Eaters

Ogygia

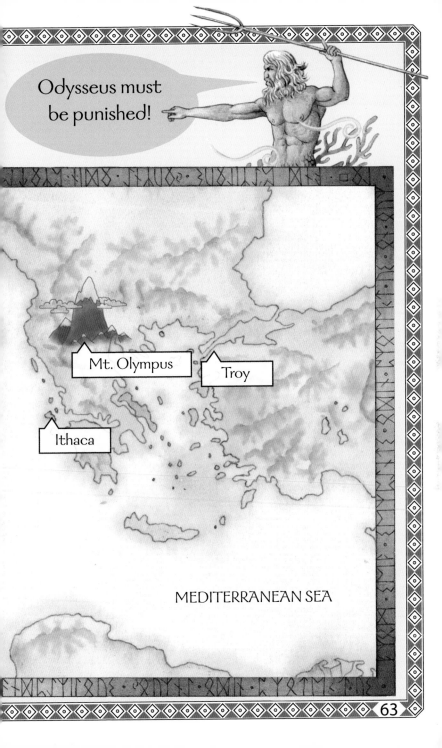

HOMER:

THE MYTH BEHIND THE MAN

Is this the man who wrote the two most important epic poems that survived from ancient Greece?

Let's investigate!

DATE:

Homer lived in the 9th or 8th century BCE and his poems are written in a style that was commonly used at that time. The ancient Greek historian Herodotus, who was alive in the 5th century BCE, claimed Homer lived only 400 years before him.

OR NOT?

Popular belief is that Homer lived just after the Trojan war (12th century BCE) and wrote about the stories he heard.

LOCATION:

He lived in Ionia (now Turkey) because his poems are mostly in the **dialect** of the Ionians.

OR NOT?

Many cities competed for the honor of having Homer as their poet. This included Smyrna and the island of Chios. It is also possible that he was located on one of the countries overlooking Troy, around the East Aegean Sea.

AUTHOR:

The Iliad and *The Odyssey* are both written in different styles. The Greek philosopher, Aristotle, suggested that this was because the two stories were written at different times in Homer's life.

OR NOT?

Some believe that the writing styles are too different to have been written by the same person. The stories were likely to have been passed down through storytellers and singers with everyone adding their own exciting twists and adaptations.

EPIC POEMS

An epic is a long story about heroic deeds written in poetry. Here are a few famous examples.

Epic of Gilgamesh

Poet: Unknown
Written: before 7th century BCE
Language: ancient Sumerian
Synopsis: the legends of a hero-king Gilgamesh, who ruled over ancient Mesopotamia (Iraq) around 27th century BCE. One of his quests included searching for immortality.

Song of the Nibelungs

Poet: unknown Austrian
Written: around 13th century
Language: German
Synopsis: the story of a dragon-slayer Siegfried who killed the chiefs of a wicked family, the Nibelungen. He captured their magic sword, their invisibility cape, and their magic gold. But the treasures were cursed.

The Iliad

Poet: Homer
Written: late 9th or early 8th century BCE
Language: ancient Greek
Synopsis: the heroic and tragic events of the 10-year siege by the Greeks against the city of Troy. The war finally came to an end when the Greeks tricked the Trojans with a huge wooden horse.

The Aeneid

Poet: Virgil
Written: 1st century BCE
Language: Latin
Synopsis: the legendary story of Aeneas who traveled from Troy to Italy. He became an ancestor of the ancient Romans.

Beowulf

Poet: Unknown
Written: between 8th and 11th centuries
Language: Old English
Synopsis: set during the 6th century, Beowulf is the son of a great warrior who helped the strong and well-loved king of Denmark. He slayed Grendel the ogre and a fiery dragon.

TROJAN WAR

Homer's epic *The Iliad* tells the story of the 10-year long Trojan War. This tale of love lost, battles won, and lessons learned warns against angering the gods and shows how cunning and creativity can triumph over physical strength.

One night the gods and goddesses are having a party. Paris, a prince of Troy, is helping to settle an argument about which goddess is the fairest. Three goddesses, Hera, Athena, and Aphrodite each offer him a bribe for the title.

Paris accepts Aphrodite's bribe of the most beautiful woman in the world: Helen. Aphrodite helps Paris steal Helen, who is married to the Greek King, **Menelaus**, and take her back to Troy.

Outraged, Menelaus gathers his troops and wages war upon Troy in a bid to win back Helen. His brother, Agamemnon, leads the Greek army and Achilles, the greatest warrior in all of Greece, fights with them.

The walls around Troy were built by the gods, Apollo and Poseidon, and are impossible to break down, no matter how hard the Greeks try. The war continues for 10 long years.

In the 10th year of the war, the Greeks make one last attempt at invading Troy. They build a large wooden horse, hide their soldiers inside it, and leave it as an offering outside Troy's gates. The Trojans bring the horse inside the city, because they believe it will bring them good luck.

The Greeks sneak out of the horse and open the gates to the rest of their army. The city of Troy falls and the Greeks win the war, and Helen. This angers the gods, who curse the Greeks, ensuring that their journey home is not an easy one.

CHAPTER 4

Thor

(Viking myths)

Are you afraid of storms, when lightning flashes, thunder rolls, and the storm clouds chase across the wild skies? Well you should be. For the hot-tempered, redheaded, hammer-wielding god Thor is riding his chariot through the heavens. Two giant goats **Tanngnjóstr** (Teeth Grinder) and **Tanngrisnir** (The Snarler) pull hard at their reins, as they race headlong through the rampaging skies. Peals of thunder boom from the wheels of the chariot.

Towering Thor with furrowed brow and

blazing eyes grips the reins in one hand, while thrashing his mighty hammer, **Mjöllnir**, in his other iron-gloved hand. Each blaze of lightning is made more dazzling by the magical strengthening power of his belt, **Megingjord**. Thor, ruler of the skies, storms, and thunder, is on his way eastward to fight the gods' main enemies, the giants, once again.

This time, Thor is after one giant in particular, **Krungnir**. Krungnir lives on the cliff-top crag, Rockyard in **Jotunheim**, the home of the mountain and frost giants. Krungnir stands waiting with his stone shield in front of him. Craftily, Thor tells a servant to inform Krungnir that he is coming from under the earth.

NORSE GOD WORLD

The Vikings were ruthless warriors, raiding countries far and wide from their native Norway, Sweden, and Denmark. Their gods and the mythical realms reflected the fearless warrior instinct of the people and the harshness of their land.

YGGDRASIL

Vikings believed a great ash tree towered over the world and its roots and branches supported the nine realms.

VANAHEIM
Land of the Vanir, or fertility gods, **Njord**, Freyja, Freyr, Idun, and Sif

JOTUNHEIM
Land of the giants

SVARTALFAHEIM OR NIDAVELLIR
Land of the dark elves (dwarfs)

MUSPELLHEIM
Land of heat and fire; this was the second world created

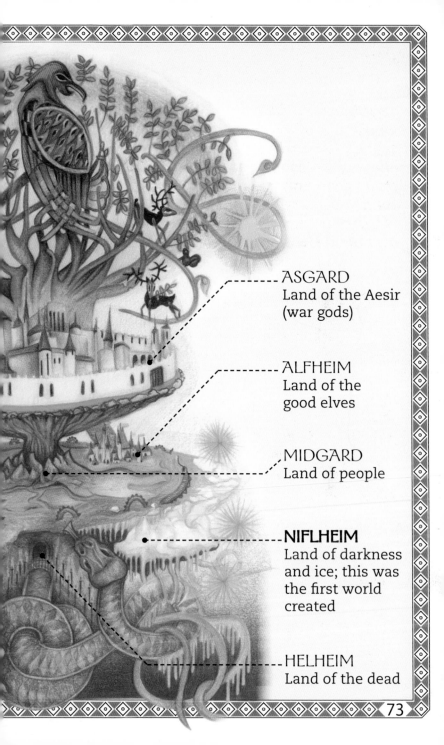

ASGARD
Land of the Aesir
(war gods)

ALFHEIM
Land of the
good elves

MIDGARD
Land of people

NIFLHEIM
Land of darkness
and ice; this was
the first world
created

HELHEIM
Land of the dead

When Krungnir receives the message, he moves his stone shield underneath his feet. Taking advantage of the lowered shield, Thor throws his hammer. It finds its target. With a single blow, the giant's skull explodes into dust. The hammer like a boomerang, continues its curve and flies back to Thor's gloved hand.

Victorious, Thor heads homeward once more. In Asgard, the realm of the war gods, he returns to his estate Thruthvangar, the Paddock of Power. There stands his great 540-roomed, golden-roofed castle, **Bilskirnir**. Here he lives with his beautiful wife Sif, the goddess of the cornfields. She has long hair made of pure gold that cascades down her back.

Ravenous after his fight, Thor sits down at his dining table to feast on a whole ox and drink three barrels of mead. He has an appetite that matches any giant's. Thor's hand reaches out and checks that his hammer is still near him. But Thor has not always had this prized possession.

One night, Thor had been away from home, hunting trolls—his favorite pastime. The mischievous god Loki could not sleep. Restless, Loki made his way to Bilskirnir, climbed a trellis and peered into the rooms.

In one room, Sif was sleeping. In spite and with a heart filled with hatred, Loki softly crept across the room, picking up some jeweled scissors and making his way to her bedside.

Quietly, he cut off all her precious golden hair, leaving just short stubble. Sif began to stir, so Loki bundled the golden locks into his tunic and hurried to the window. As he climbed out, one of his sandals fell off but he had no time to retrieve it.

Sif shrieked and wailed when she saw her reflection. When Thor returned and saw his wife, he was furious. He recognized the sandal as belonging to Loki and went to find him.

Through chattering teeth, Loki begged for his life, promising gifts for the gods in return. Thor let him go.

Loki made his way to Svartalfaheim, the world of the dark elves. He was owed a favor by a tribe of dwarfs. All dwarfs are skilled craftsmen, making things from the gold, silver, and gems they mine. Loki requested them to make the finest head of golden hair, a spear named **Gungnir** for Odin (god of war), and a magical ship, Skidblade, for Freyja (goddess of magic).

?

QUESTION
Why did Loki
cut Sif's hair?

?

NORSE GODS FAMILY TREE

Vikings held their gods in high esteem and bestowed them with great honor and respect. There are two types of gods in Norse mythology: the Aesir, gods of war who live in Asgard, and the Vanir, gods of fertility who live in Vanaheim. Here are some of them.

FRIGG
Goddess of marriage and motherhood

NJORD
God of wind and sea

Married

SKADI
Goddess of skiing and hunting

HODER
A blind, very strong god
He was fooled by the trickster god Loki into killing his brother Balder.

FREYJA
Goddess of love, beauty, and magic

FREYR
God of peace, sunshine, and prosperity

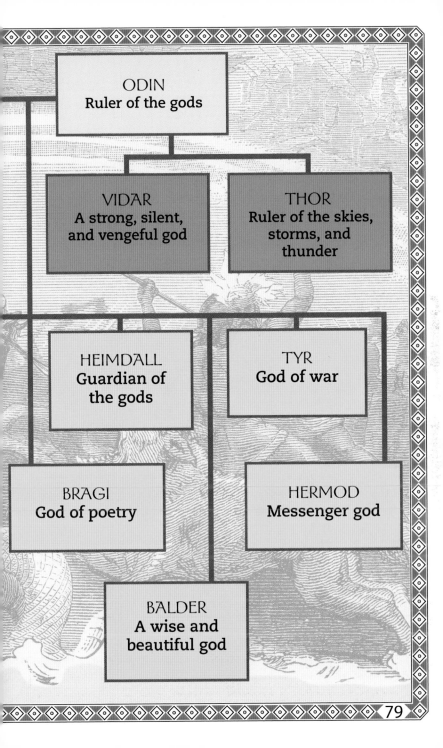

ODIN
Ruler of the gods

VIDAR
A strong, silent, and vengeful god

THOR
Ruler of the skies, storms, and thunder

HEIMDALL
Guardian of the gods

TYR
God of war

BRAGI
God of poetry

HERMOD
Messenger god

BALDER
A wise and beautiful god

As Loki returned, he passed the blacksmith forge of two famous dwarfs, Brokk and Sindri. Feeling mischievous, Loki made a bet with them. "I'll wager my head that you can't make three treasures as good as these I have already."

Brokk and Sindri set to work. Brokk pumped the bellows of the furnace as Sindri crafted.

Loki, realizing that he might lose the bet, changed into a horsefly and attempted to distract Brokk by biting him. But despite the pain, Brokk kept pumping. The first treasure was a live golden boar, Gullinbursti, the second a golden ring, **Draupnir**, and the

third a magical hammer, Mjöllnir. They were perfect and Loki had lost the bet.

However, the dwarfs could not cut off Loki's head, for this would mean severing his neck, which was not in the wager. Instead they sewed together Loki's lips so the god could cause no more mischief with his words.

Thor was powerful with his hammer and greatly feared by all, but the end time **Ragnarok** will one day approach. On that day, a rooster will mark the start of the great battle. The gods with their army of heroes, will fight the giants and their army of undead, led by Fenrir, the wolf from the Underworld, and **Jormungander**, the World Serpent.

THE RAGNAROK RUMBLE

AESIR vs. JOTUNS

Choose your side and take your seat—the great battle of Ragnarok is about to commence!

BOOM!

ZA

In the blue corner, fighting for the side of the gods (Aesir) are:

The Valkyries
These female deities are the handmaidens of Odin and are courageous fighters.

The Einherjar
These are the soldiers who died in previous battles. They rise again to fight at Ragnarok.

The Berserkers
These terrifying warriors wear wolf or bear skins to scare their opponents. They are ferocious fighters who don't feel pain.

Heimdall
Heimdall has an old score to settle with Loki. He once stopped Loki from stealing Freyja's necklace and there has been bad blood between the pair ever since.

POW!

Overview

Thor and Loki were blood brothers until Loki caused the death of Balder. Odin imprisoned Loki for this crime and evil descended upon the world. Loki became bitter and when released, he called upon his band of monsters and waged war upon the gods…

WHAM!

In the red corner, fighting for the side of the giants (Jotuns) are:

Surt
This fire giant is destined to kill Freyr at Ragnarok. Surt, along with two humans will be the only beings to survive the battle.

Fenrir
This wolf is a huge, savage beast who spent years chained to a rock. At Ragnarok, he will break his chains, wreak havoc, and eat Odin.

Jormungander
This scary serpent lives in the ocean that surrounds Midgard. At Ragnarok, the beast is pitted against its **nemesis**, the mighty Thor.

Referee's verdict

Both good and evil will be destroyed in this battle, but all is not lost. The Earth will rise again and the human couple will start a new world without the taint of evil.

Thor had once before nearly succeeded in destroying Jormungander on a fishing trip with the giant Hymir. Thor had successfully trapped the World Serpent using an ox's head as bait. As the Serpent had writhed, the boat had rocked and, in fear, Hymir had cut the fishing line before Thor could bring down his hammer. The World Serpent escaped.

At Ragnarok, the World Serpent will stir up tidal waves and smother the Earth and sky with thick smoky clouds of poisonous breath. Thor will find himself caught in the writhing coils of the Serpent's body, gasping by this strangle-hold and the fumes. Thor's hammer will not fail him though. The lightning will strike the Serpent's heart and the beast will collapse. Released from the coils, Thor will sink down too, choked to death by the poisonous mist.

Ragnarok, the "Twilight of the Gods," is the fatal day when most of the gods are destined to die. It is when the lands of the gods, the elves, the giants, and the people will burn, and the universe, no longer protected by the gods, returns to its original chaos of nothingness.

FABLE TOWN POLICE EVIDENCE ROOM

AUTHORIZED PERSONNEL ONLY

Welcome, detective. Please feel free to look around. Each item has already been bagged and tagged but please wear gloves when touching them. Handle with care, these weapons are very dangerous and some even have mystical powers.

MJÖLLNIR
Description: large hammer belonging to Norse god Thor. The hammer never misses its mark and always returns itself to the thrower's hand.

EXCALIBUR
Description: sword belonging to English King Arthur. Given to him by the mysterious "Lady of the Lake," it is often thought to have magical powers.

TRIDENT

Description: trident belonging to Poseidon. It holds the power of the seas and can be used to stir up storms, shake the ground, and even create new islands from the seabed.

GUNGNIR

Description: spear belonging to Norse god Odin. This spear is perfectly balanced and always hits its mark and kills its victim, regardless of how skilled the thrower is.

THUNDERBOLT

Description: thunderbolt belonging to Zeus. This weapon has the power to make the whole sky shake. It has precision aim and can be used to kill an opponent or to shatter their weapon.

MIDGARD DAILY WEATHER REPORT

Here is what the Norse gods have in store for us in the next five days.

"Expect to see the many faces of fall this week with a mixture of sunshine and showers. We must thank Freyr, god of sunshine, for smiling down on us and bringing warm temperatures and blue skies.

Leading into Wednesday, there will be a cold front moving westward and the threat of showers throughout the day. Thor must be swinging his hammer because thunder and lightning will be charging across the sky.

By Friday morning, the gods will be in a terrible mood and a hurricane will be heading inland. Severe weather warnings are expected. People are urged to pray to Njord, god of wind and sea, to encourage calmer weather for next week."

Pressure map

Five-day forecast

Mon	Tues	Wed	Thurs	Fri
59°F	57°F	51°F	51°F	50°F
15°C	14°C	11°C	11°C	10°C

MONSTROUS
MURALS

Welcome to the gallery of the giants. Here are some of the most famous giants of myths and legends. To your right is Jack's Giant, the hulking bone-cruncher himself. To your left is Ymir, the glacial gigantor who will be sure to give you the chills. Browse around the gallery to learn more about each of these colossal characters.

Ymir

Ymir was the first of the Nordic frost giants. He was a huge and monstrous being and, when he was killed, his body was used to create Midgard (the Earth). His flesh became the soil, his blood turned into the rivers, and his bones formed the mountains.

Rübezahl

This shape-shifting giant from German legend was called the "Hey-Hey" man. His echoing cries could make travelers become lost in the forest and if they mocked him they could end up losing their lives.

Jack's Giant

This people-eating giant from the classic fairy tale *Jack and the Beanstalk* is famous for saying "Fee-Fi-Fo-Fum! I smell the blood of an Englishman." Jack meets the giant after climbing up a huge beanstalk.

Atlas

Atlas was one of the great Greek Titans. He led the Titans in a rebellion against the sky god, Zeus. Defeated, he was sentenced by Zeus to hold the heavens upon his shoulders for eternity.

CHAPTER 5

Monkey King's Mischief
(Chinese myths)

A long, long time ago, and far, far away, a large stone perched at the peak of a very high mountain. Energized by the warm rays from Earth and Heaven, and fertilized by the force of the wind, the stone magically transformed into an egg.

CRACK! As the stone egg broke, a fully grown monkey stepped out. Its eyes shone with radiant golden light.

In the heavenly court of the immortals, the Jade Emperor, ruler of Heaven and Earth, saw the bright light. "What's causing that?" he asked his chief priest.

After investigating, the chief priest reported back. "The light came from a monkey that hatched from a stone, but it has now eaten food like a mortal and the light is fading."

"Just a monkey," replied the Jade Emperor, relieved. "Now let us get back to our more important work."

In another part of Heaven, Lord **Lao Tzu**, Supreme **Patriarch** of the Taoists, was purifying the potion of everlasting life. A ray reached his laboratory. "The one who made that light will surely become immortal," Tzu thought.

In Paradise, the Buddha was talking to his followers when he also noticed the bright light shine into his temple. Buddha paused, meditated, and then said, "A remarkable creature has just been born who is destined to become a true Buddha."

The monkey came down from the mountain and met the island's monkeys. He led them to a hidden cave behind a waterfall where they could live safely. The monkeys honored him by making him their king.

On his 400th birthday, the Monkey King feasted with the monkeys, but he was gloomy. "I'm only 400 years old, but I've already reached the greatest rank as king. Is there nothing more to strive for?"

"Kings are not the highest beings, Your Majesty," answered a gibbon. "There are gods who live in Heaven and rule Earth, powerful immortals who live forever, and wise Buddhas who have reached perfect **enlightenment**."

"Marvelous!" cried the Monkey King. "I will aim to become all three, starting with immortal."

The next morning, Monkey boarded a raft and sailed away from the island across the great ocean. On his journey, he stopped at lands where he gathered human clothes—black

boots, a red robe, and a yellow sash. He was
guided to the Divine Cave of the Three Stars
in the side of the Mountain of Heart and Mind.
Before he could knock, the door was opened
by a young man.

"My master, Patriarch Subodhi, told me to let you in because you wish to study the Way," said the young man. He led Monkey to a large room where the Patriarch sat cross-legged in the center surrounded by students. The Patriarch looked very old, yet strong and alert, with a long beard trailing behind him.

Monkey worked hard and listened eagerly, learning from the **Taoist** priest. After seven years, Monkey needed further challenges. The Patriarch taught Monkey how to transform himself into 72 forms. It didn't take long for clever Monkey to master that. Then Monkey was taught to travel on clouds, leaping thousands of miles in a single somersault. After only another three months, the agile Monkey had mastered that. Finally, the Patriarch told Monkey the secrets of Eternal Life. For three years, Monkey practiced.

One day, Monkey was sitting outside the cave with the other students. "Can you really change into something else?" a student asked Monkey.

"Yes, watch this!" Monkey exclaimed, and changed himself into a unicorn. The students were impressed and applauded Monkey as he bowed. On hearing the noise, the Patriarch summoned Monkey.

"Showing off has put you in great danger," said the Patriarch. "You must leave, and you will need to find a weapon to protect yourself. I suggest you go to the Dragon King of the Eastern Seas."

Monkey thanked the Patriarch and then somersaulted into the air, traveling from cloud to cloud.

The Dragon King lived in a jade palace at the bottom of the sea and was surprised to see Monkey being ushered into the throne room by a guard.

"I need a magic weapon to match my abilities," requested Monkey.

The Dragon King showed him several magical swords and axes from his treasure store. Monkey wielded them and swung them around, but each time complained that they were too light, and even broke a few. This further surprised the Dragon King for they were the heaviest weapons in the palace.

The Dragon Queen entered and suggested an immovable giant pillar of iron, which once belonged to Yu the Great to control floods. The 20-foot-long, thick pillar was too heavy to be brought out so Monkey was taken to see it. As Monkey approached, the pillar glowed. He grasped the pillar with both hands and lifted it to the amazement of the Dragon King.

"If only it were smaller," Monkey wished. Obediently the pillar shrank. Shorter and shorter, thinner and thinner, the pillar shrank until Monkey was able to hold it easily, yet it still was the same heavy weight.

"A perfect staff!" exclaimed Monkey. "Grow!" he then commanded. The pillar increased in size to more than 100 feet high. The Dragon King's palace shook as Monkey tried out his new weapon. The waters of the seas swirled in confusion. The magical dragons of the four seas arose.

"Stop!" they cried.

"Not until you give me three further gifts," replied Monkey, "cloud-walking boots, the phoenix-feather cap, and the golden armor."

A battle ensued. Despite the power of the dragons, Monkey defeated them with his skills and his powerful weapon.

"Take the gifts," said the dragons. Monkey instructed the pillar to shrink, and left, taking with him the magical possessions.

Stretching himself out upon a rock near the sea, Monkey rested. As he drifted into sleep, Monkey felt himself dragged to his feet by two figures—one with a horse's head and the other with an ox's head.

"Where are you taking me? How did I get here?" Monkey asked, looking around. There was no sight of the sea, but instead the land was barren and dark.

QUESTION
What were the three gifts Monkey wanted?

Monkey and his two guards approached the gate of a walled city. Fully awake now, Monkey exclaimed, "It's the Land of the Dead. I don't belong here!"

Monkey seized his staff from its hiding place behind his ear. "Grow!" he commanded, and the pillar shot up. The guards fled.

Swinging the staff, Monkey entered the city and advanced to the Palace of Lord Yama, the Lord of the Dead.

"I cannot be dead because I am immortal," claimed Monkey as he stood before Yama and the nine Judges of the Dead. "Let me see the Register of Life and Death," he demanded.

In the Hall of Darkness, the dusty volumes of the register were brought out. Monkey found his name and, dipping a writing brush into some ink, then blotted out his name.

"This cannot be allowed!" protested Yama, but he was helpless against Monkey's powerful staff. Monkey slammed the book shut and left the palace. As he walked back out of the city gate, he found himself back on the rock surrounded by sea.

Looking up to the sky, Monkey said to himself, "Now that I've achieved immortality, I'll go to Heaven and become a god."

When Monkey arrived in Heaven, the Jade Emperor had already received complaints about him from the Dragon King of the Eastern Sea and Lord Yama. Seeking advice, the Jade Emperor decided to give Monkey a position in Heaven so that he could keep an eye on the mischief-maker. The role was to oversee the care of the heavenly horses in the Imperial Stables. Monkey accepted and got to work, believing this to be a high-ranking position.

However, when Monkey discovered he had actually been given a low post, he caused havoc at a grand heavenly banquet. The Jade Emperor was horrified. Twelve Thunder Generals attempted to defeat Monkey in a ferocious battle, but Monkey outclassed them with his skills. Monkey could create other monkeys just from the hairs on his tail.

Kwan Yin, Most Compassionate **Bodhisattva**, stepped forward. With just a porcelain vase in her hands, she rose into the air and taking aim, dropped it onto Monkey's head. Monkey collapsed unconscious.

"Execute him," commanded the Jade Emperor.

"That will not be possible," replied Lord Lao Tzu. "He ate too many Pills of Immortality at the banquet so his body will be as hard as diamond and no weapon will be able to cut through. Let me heat him in my sacred cauldron where the flames can even burn up immortals."

Monkey found himself in the dark when he awoke, rubbing his sore head. As he groped around, he could feel the scorching heat from the sides of the porcelain pot. Instead of burning him, the heat strengthened Monkey further because he had been born of rock.

In a rage, Monkey reached behind his ear for his staff. "Grow!" The staff instantly lengthened, shattering the cauldron. Released, Monkey stormed to the heavenly court and demanded that the Jade Emperor give up the throne to him. In desperation, the Jade Emperor sent for the help of Buddha, the wisest of all.

"Why do you think you should rule Heaven and Earth?" the Buddha asked Monkey.

"Because I have great powers," boasted Monkey.

The Buddha challenged Monkey to jump off the palm of his hand. Monkey accepted and leaped. He landed in an empty space with just five pillars. Thinking this was the edge of the universe, Monkey marked the central pillar

as proof. After leaping back, he looked down
at Buddha's hand and saw his middle finger
marked. Buddha had transformed his hand
and Monkey had never left his palm. Monkey
had lost the challenge and was imprisoned
under a magic mountain to repent for all
the chaos he had caused.

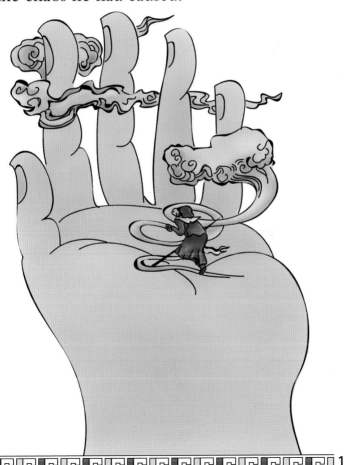

Five hundred years later, a gentle priest called **Xuanzang** was required to travel west to India to bring the Buddhists' sacred scrolls back to China. Knowing that there would be many dangers on the journey, he needed to find some companions to protect him. Monkey was the perfect choice.

Finally released, Monkey willingly joined the humble priest. Two others also joined the group: an exiled general, Sha Wujing, and a banished commander, **Zhu Euneng**, who had been transformed into a pig.

As they traveled through imaginary lands, the companions were tested by many dangers. On one adventure, they noticed the air getting hotter and hotter. The Fiery Mountains were ahead of them. The only way across was with a special plantain fan, which belonged to Princess Iron Fan.

Monkey stood before the princess and requested her fan. She refused and waved it, causing Monkey to blow away.

The second time, Monkey went with a wind-fixing pill in his mouth. The princess again refused his request but Monkey stood firm when she tried to wave the fan.

This time, the princess locked herself away, but Monkey transformed into an insect and flew into her room. He landed in the tea that she was drinking, and as she sipped, the princess swallowed the insect. From inside, Monkey caused her great pain until she agreed to give him the fan. She did so, but she gave him a false fan.

The third time, Monkey transformed himself into the princess's husband, the Bull Demon King. She did not refuse the request this time. As she passed the fan to Monkey, the actual Bull Demon King appeared, and chased Monkey. They fought fiercely and Sha Wujing and Pig joined in to help in the fight.

Eventually winning, Monkey was able to fan the Demon's fire as they crossed the Fiery Mountains to escape. This was one of many adventures on the quest to retrieve the sacred scrolls.

Returning successfully, the four companions were all rewarded by becoming Buddhas for

they had reached the state of enlightenment.
They had earned their position in Heaven.
Monkey had achieved his ambitions.

?
QUESTION
What were Monkey's
three ambitions?
?

PROVERBS

Many cultures have their own proverbs or sayings. Proverbs are short sentences about a common belief or piece of advice. They are often metaphorical, which means that they will describe a subject by comparing it to something different. Here are some examples of proverbs.

Look before you leap.

Every cloud has a silver lining.

Practice what you preach.

Actions speak louder than words.

The early bird gets the worm.

Learn from past mistakes to avoid future ones.

Things at their worst will mend.

A smile can erase a million worries.

A bad word whispered echoes a hundred miles.

Every step leaves its print.

CHINESE DRAGONS

Huan ying! Welcome! I am one of the great, mythical Chinese dragons. My fellow dragons and I are very wise and extremely powerful. Chinese people hold us in high esteem and rightly so. We can control water and will create great floods if we are angered—we dragons have very short tempers! However, we are charitable creatures and the rains that we bring allow crops to grow. In return, we simply ask that we be worshipped. Chinese people know that if they do not, then they will feel our wrath!

NUMBER NINE

In Chinese culture, I am associated with the lucky number nine. The number nine is favored because it sounds similar to the Chinese word that means "long lasting." I resemble parts from nine other creatures and also have nine children.

9

九

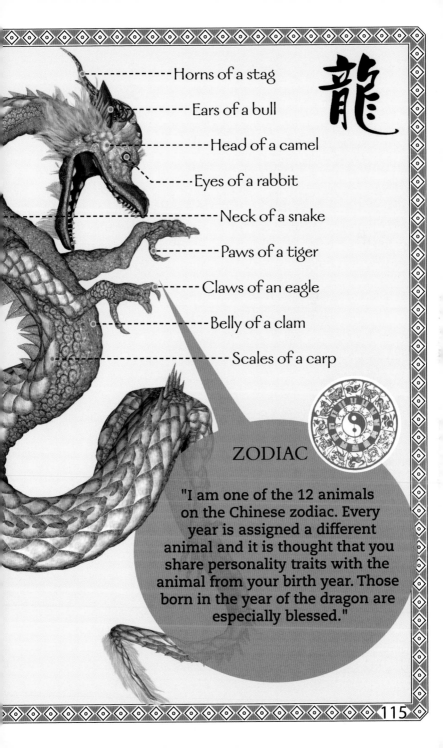

Horns of a stag

Ears of a bull

Head of a camel

Eyes of a rabbit

Neck of a snake

Paws of a tiger

Claws of an eagle

Belly of a clam

Scales of a carp

龍

ZODIAC

"I am one of the 12 animals on the Chinese zodiac. Every year is assigned a different animal and it is thought that you share personality traits with the animal from your birth year. Those born in the year of the dragon are especially blessed."

MONKEY KING BOARD GAME

Join the Monkey King on his quest for enlightenment. Play in pairs or groups. Place game pieces at the start of the path. Take turns to roll a die and move your piece. The first person to reach the end wins. Just keep your wits about you—there will be many obstacles in your way on the long road to Heaven!

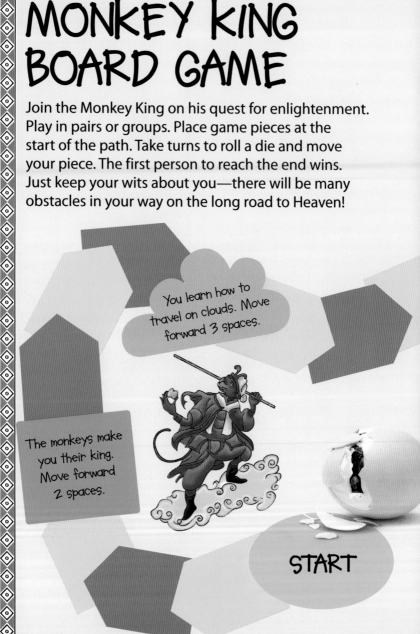

You learn how to travel on clouds. Move forward 3 spaces.

The monkeys make you their king. Move forward 2 spaces.

START

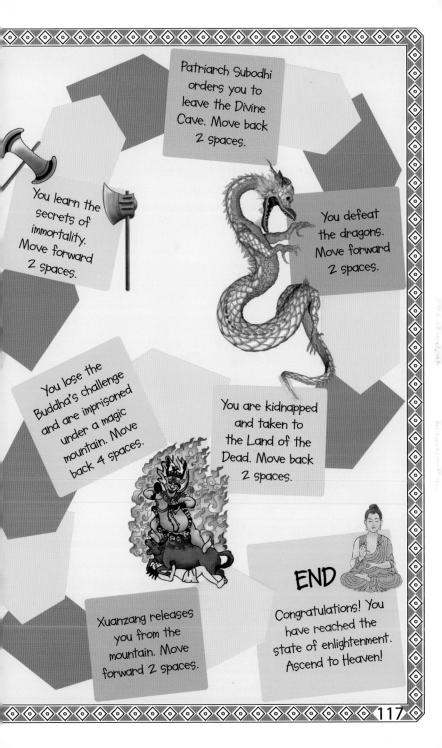

Patriarch Subodhi orders you to leave the Divine Cave. Move back 2 spaces.

You learn the secrets of immortality. Move forward 2 spaces.

You defeat the dragons. Move forward 2 spaces.

You lose the Buddha's challenge and are imprisoned under a magic mountain. Move back 4 spaces.

You are kidnapped and taken to the Land of the Dead. Move back 2 spaces.

Xuanzang releases you from the mountain. Move forward 2 spaces.

END

Congratulations! You have reached the state of enlightenment. Ascend to Heaven!

CHINESE OPERA:
The Art of the Mask

For generations myths have been told and passed down in many different ways. In China, one of these ways is through the art of Chinese Opera.

Chinese Opera is one of the oldest dramatic art forms in the world and is still a very popular pastime for many Chinese people. The shows combine music, literature, and art. Actors will often wear colorful masks or paint their faces with distinctive designs.

The extravagant masks and paints help the audience to identify the characters and will often symbolize their personality traits.

THE MAIN MASK COLORS AND THEIR MEANINGS ARE:

RED
Courage, intelligence, and bravery

PURPLE
Wisdom, justice, and sophistication

BLACK
Loyalty and selflessness

WHITE
Trickery and evil

YELLOW
Cruelty and ferocity

MAKE YOUR OWN MONKEY KING MASK

Use a paper plate and cut two slits at the top and bottom. Curve the plate to make a face shape and glue or staple the slits together. Cut out some monkey ears, a nose, and eye holes. Draw a monkey face on the plate like the design here.

SPINNING A YARN:
HOW TO TELL A STORY

Many myths and legends would have been lost years ago, if it were not for skilled storytellers keeping them alive. With a little imagination and inspiration, anyone can become a storyteller. Here are a few tips to help get you started.

- Get some inspiration. Watch, read, and listen to other stories. They will give you good ideas for how to present yours.

- Practice makes perfect. Rehearse your story to make sure you know it very well.

- Set the scene. When starting your story, describe the setting and introduce the main characters.

- Use props. Costumes, sets, and props add a visual element to your story.

- Use your voice. Changing the tone of your voice helps to create an atmosphere and build tension, making your story more exciting.

- Engage your audience. Make eye contact with your audience members so they feel as though you are speaking directly to them.

- Take your time. Don't rush through your story. If you keep a steady pace it will be easier for your audience to follow the narrative. You can also take longer pauses for dramatic effect.

- Keep the story flowing. Ensure that your narrative makes sense and that you are not jumping from one section of the story to another.

- Have a clear ending. Close the story when the battle has been won or the journey completed.

- Ask your audience questions. Start a discussion about the characters, events, or ideas in the story.

Get ready to start unraveling a story. Wrap your audience up in thrilling legends of terrifying monsters, cunning tricksters, and magical gods. There are thousands of stories waiting to be told—where will you begin?

MYTHS QUIZ

See if you can remember the answers to these questions about what you have read.

1. How did Raven's feathers become black in the North American myth?

2. What did Raven take from the Sky Chief?

3. What are the names of Odin's two ravens?

4. What creature is Kitsune?

5. How did Anansi capture Python?

6. What is the name of the deceitful Norse god?

7. Where was Odysseus sailing home to?

8. Why was Poseidon angry with Odysseus?

9. What is the name of the ancient Greek Underworld?

10. Who is said to be the author of the epic poems *The Iliad* and *The Odyssey*?

11. What event is told about in *The Iliad*?

12. What is the name of the land of the Norse war gods?

13. Who made Thor's hammer, Mjöllnir?

14. What is the name of the Norse battle that brings the end of time?

15. What was Thor's nemesis?

16. What was Monkey King's weapon?

17. Why did Monkey King not die in the sacred cauldron?

18. Complete this proverb: every cloud has a. . .?

Answers on page 124.

GLOSSARY

BCE
Time before the common era, or year zero.

Bodhisattva
Person who follows the way of life of a Buddha.

Dialect
Regional type of language that has certain features of vocabulary and pronunciation.

Enlightenment
Final state reached when a person is blessed and has no desire or suffering.

Immortal
Can live forever.

Nemesis
Long-standing enemy.

Nymphs
Gods represented as beautiful women.

Patriarch
Man who is a father or founder.

Plantation
Large piece of land where one crop is grown.

Sorceress
Woman who practices sorcery or magic.

Taoist
Person who seeks harmony by following the Chinese customs of the Tao.

Totem
Object that symbolizes a family or group of people.

Answers to the Myths Quiz:
1. They were scorched by flames; **2.** A magic ball of light;
3. Huginn and Muninn; **4.** A shape-shifting nine-tailed fox;
5. Python laid along a branch to measure itself; **6.** Loki;
7. Ithaca; **8.** Odysseus and his crew had hurt Poseidon's son Polyphemus; **9.** Hades; **10.** Homer; **11.** The Trojan War;
12. Asgard; **13.** The dwarfs Brokk and Sindri; **14.** Ragnarok;
15. Jormungander, the World Serpent; **16.** Length-changing pillar of iron; **17.** Monkey was born of rock; **18.** Silver lining.

PRONUNCIATION GUIDE

Achilles
[uh-KIL-leez]

Aegisthus
[ee-JIS-thus]

Aeolia
[EE-oh-li-ah]

Agamemnon
[ag-ah-MEM-non]

Bilskirnir
[BILL-skeer-neer]

Charybdis
[CAR-ib-dis]

Draupnir
[droop-NIR]

Einherjar
[ayn-HER-yar]

Gungnir
[GUNG-neer]

Jormungander
[yur-MAN-gan-der]

Jotunheim
[YOT-un-haym]

Krungnir
[KROO-ng-neer]

Lord Lao Tzu
[lord LOW zu]

Megingjord
[meg-ing-YORD]

Menelaus
[men-UH-lay-uhs]

Mjöllnir
[mee-YOL-neer]

Muspellheim
[MOOSE-spell-haym]

Niflheim
[neef-LE-haym]

Njord
[YORD]

Nyame
[knee-YA-may]

Odin
[OO-den]

Odysseus
[oh-DIS-ee-uhs]

Ogygia
[OH-jee-jee-ah]

Polyphemus
[poly-FEE-mus]

Poseidon
[poss-EYE-don]

Ragnarok
[rang-NAR-erk]

Svartalfaheim
[svart-al-FA-haym]

Tanngnjóstr
[TAN-yost-er]

Tanngrisnir
[tan-GRIS-neer]

Telepylus
[te-lep-EE-lus]

Tiresias
[tire-ee-SEE-uhs]

Valkyrie
[val-KEE-ree]

Xuanzang
[SHWAN-zang]

Yggdrasil
[ig-DRA-seel]

Zhu Euneng
[chu YOO-neng]

INDEX

About the Author

Deborah Lock is Senior Editor at DK, as well as a writer and mother of two. She was previously a teacher and has worked at DK since 1998, producing children's nonfiction books about all kinds of topics, from history, science, and politics to art, music, gardening, pirates, and mythical beasts. She is the series editor of the *DK Readers* reading program and is currently working on some innovative new products for the best-selling educational *Made Easy* workbooks program. She spends her leisure time involved with youth work and has a passion for singing, drama, and dancing.

About the Consultant

Dr. Linda Gambrell, Distinguished Professor of Education at Clemson University, has served as President of the National Reading Conference, the College Reading Association, and the International Reading Association. She is also reading consultant for the *DK Readers*.

Have you read these other great books from DK?

DK ADVENTURES

Discover the fascinating world of creepy-crawlies in the Amazon.

Relive the drama of famous shipwrecks and survivors' stories.

Encounter the rare animals in the mountain forests of Cambodia.

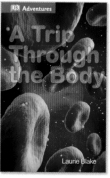

Be a rock detective! Look up close at rocks, minerals, and sparkling gems.

Explore the amazing systems at work inside the human body.

Step back nearly 20,000 years to the days of early cave dwellers.